The Wonderful Hebrew
עִבְרִית
Alphabet 1
Workbook

TARVER ELITE PUBLISHING

The Rev. Dr. Tracey Tarver

Printed in the United States of America

First Printing, 2021

Follow Rev. Tracey Tarver on social media

Facebook: Pekudei Learning Center

Publishing Company: Tarver Elite Publishing

ISBN: 978-1-5136-8222-8

TABLE OF CONTENTS

IT IS FORBIDDEN TO READ GOD'S WORD OR STUDY THE HEBREW SCRIPTURES WITHOUT PRAYING

BEFORE THE READING

Baruch Atah Adonai, elo-heinu melech ha-olam, asher bachar banu mi-kol ha-amim v'natan lanu et Torah-to. Baruch Atah Adonai, noten ha-Torah.

Blessed are You, Adonai our God, Ruler of the universe, who has chosen us from among all the nations, and given us the Torah. Blessed are You, Adonai, Provider of the Torah.

AFTER THE READING

Baruch Atah Adonai, elo-heinu melech ha-olam, asher natan lanu Torat emet, v'cha-yei olam nata b'tocheinu. Baruch Atah Adonai, noten ha-Torah.

Blessed are You, Adonai our God, Ruler of the universe, who has given us the

Torah of truth, and implanted within us eternal life. Blessed are You, Adonai, Provider of the Torah.

I would like to take this time to define some words used in this book from a Messianic perspective. Sometimes we approach a new teaching with an understanding formed by all our previous religious affiliations. As strange as it is, many times these previous exposures have unbeknown to us planted seeds of prejudice against the very people of God that He has admonished us to be joined with. To uncover and clear some of these hidden seeds we need to look at these words at the onset of the course.

JEW = A word representing those who come from the tribe of Judah

Hebrew = to describe those who are descended from Shem Eber. Eber was a place more than a person meaning the land beyond and is the land that was occupied the longest.

Therefore, they were called the "Eberews". It has come to mean "Those who have crossed over…"

YAHSHUAH = Hebrew name meaning 'Savior' and the Biblical name for the Greek name Jesus. Formally called Yahshuah Ha Mashiac.

REPLACEMENT THEOLOGY - The teaching of these last days that takes the Biblical promises of Israel and assigns them to the church. The church has been grafted in, adopted into Israel and therefore we shall be one, Jews and Gentiles.

YOU ARE ABOUT TO
EMBARK ON THE
GREATEST JOURNEY OF
YOUR LIFE....

THE HEBREW ALPHABET

READ EACH ROW FROM RIGHT TO LEFT

Teit	Cheit	Zayin	Vav	Hei	Dalet	Gimel	Beit	Alef
(T)	(Ch)	(Z)	(V/O/U)	(H)	(D)	(G)	(B/V)	(Silent)
Samekh	Nun	Nun	Mem	Mem	Lamed	Khaf	Kaf	Yod
(S)	(N)	(N)	(M)	(M)	(L)	(Kh)	(K/Kh)	(Y)
Tav	Shin	Reish	Qof	Tzadei	Tzadei	Fe	Pei	Ayin
(T/S)	(Sh/S)	(R)	(Q)	(Tz)	(Tz)	(F)	(P/F)	(Silent)

CHAPTER 1

THE WONDERS OF BIBLICAL HEBREW

HOLY! HOLY! HOLY!

1.1

Hi, we're tablet buddies! We are here to help you through your first part of the journey in learning the Wonders of the Hebrew alphabet.

So let's get started!

The first thing we need to understand is that Biblical Hebrew is:

Lashon HaKodesh meaning **The Holy Tongue.**

Lashon means Tongue & **Kodesh** means Holy…. **Ha** means 'The'

So-o-o   put it all together we have

'TONGUE THE HOLY'

Flip it around so it makes sense to us westerners and it is **The Holy Tongue.**

Getting a good understanding of "Holy" is important at the onset of this Journey because God is a Holy God.

Today people have assigned many meanings to the word Holy. List 5 things that come to mind when you hear the word.

1. _____

2. _____

3. _____

4. _____

5. _____

INVOLVEMENT NOT ASCETICISM

Usually, one of the first words that come to mind when we mention "Holy" is separate. Although that is part of the definition it is far from complete.

Some faiths build themselves on being separate from everything and chastising or denying the body of pleasures. This is sometimes called "Asceticism" and is a Greek word meaning exercise or training. While exercise and training are important, asceticism is a lifestyle absent from worldly pleasures to pursue spiritual goals.

What's wrong with that??? (Your opinion)

_____

_____

_____

_____

_____

_____

_____

Kodesh (Holy) implies separation from and joining unto. Remember the account of creation, what did God do?

He separated and joined…separated from and joined unto like kind and like mind.

One became two…became one! Let me say that again. One became two…the two became one.

That gives us a clearer understanding of the word **'Holy'**. It is separated from and joined to.

A distinction must be made between Gods' approach and the secular approach to any situation

On another level "Kodesh" means:

'A LEVEL ABOVE OUR HUMAN FRAME OF REFERENCE TO GOD-LIKENESS'

We will cover more levels of the word 'Holy' as we study the letters of God's language, but for now we understand two things.

1. Biblical Hebrew is called_____.

2. Which means_____.

Biblical Hebrew is Holy because it is the language of the Bible and the language the prophets spoke.

It is separate from, beyond, and different than any of the other languages of the world.

Notes:_____

_____

_____

ALTHOUGH THERE ARE NUMEROUS LEVELS AND DEMINSIONS TO EACH LETTER OF THE HEBREW ALPHABET, THE APPROACH OF THIS BOOK IS TOWARDS:

1. The Letter.

2. The Construction.

3. The Numerical Value.

4. Their Meanings As Words.

5. Their Pictorial Symbol.

EACH LETTER HAS INTRINSIC MEANING AND IS NOT ONLY A SYMBOL WITH AN AGREED UPON MEANING AS IN OTHER LANGUAGES.

THE POSTIONS AND ORDER OF THE LETTERS ARE BY DIVINE DESIGN. THE CONSTRUCTION AND NUMERICAL VALUE GIVE REVELATION INTO THE ESSENCE OF THE THING FOR WHICH THAT LETTER IS PART OF THE THREE LETTER ROOT. THE PICTORAL SYMBOLS GIVE FURTHER INSIGHT.

Notes:

THERE ARE 26 CONSONANTS IN THE HEBREW ALPHABET. THIS CAN BE FURTHER UNDERSTOOD BY THE FACT THAT THERE ARE 22 LETTERS, 5 ENDTIME (SOFIT) LETTERS WHICH TOTALS 27 YET ALEPH IS CONSIDERED HOLY AND STANDS ALONE WHICH EQUALS 26.

THE WONDERFUL HEBREW ALPHABET 1 WORKBOOK WILL STUDY LETTERS ALEPH THRU ZAYIN.

HEBREW DOES NOT HAVE A SEPARATE NUMBERING SYSTEM, BUT LETTERS HAVE NUMERICAL VALUE.

ALEPH = 1

BEIT = 2

GIMMEL = 3

DALET = 4

HEH = 5

VAV = 6

ZAYIN = 7

"All things were made by Him; and without him was not anything made that was made."
John 1:3

Now Let's see how Hebrew words are built

1.2

Biblical Hebrew uses a two or three letter root to build words that **represents a concept and speaks of the essence of a thing.**

We are studying Lashon HaKodesh....Biblical Hebrew.

Everyday Hebrew language is not Lashon HaKodesh.

Each Individual letter is called an Oat, or sometimes written "Ot" **Oat means sign**... It is saying something.

Essence is defined as the intrinsic nature of something that determines its character. The quality or qualities that make a thing what it is.

ESSENCE IS THE QUALITY THAT MAKES A THING WHAT IT IS

What makes a dog a dog? That's essence What makes a ruby a ruby? That's essence.

What makes a Persian cat different from a Lion? That's essence.

Adam was given the ability to name the animals by understanding their **essence, _their spiritual root._**

- Dog - Ke'lav (Khaf-Lamed- Vav) meaning "Like Heart."

- The World (Land) - Eretz from root word retz mean "I run", " I move."

- The World on a spiritual level means Olam from the word Elam meaning "Hidden."

- Kaph is a hand(palm),

- Samek– means support, Aleph refers of above and below.

- So KISE', (chair) is an object, **a hand that supports from above and below**.

- Midabair (to speak) Mem= from, dalet = door, beit = house (Ba) = in, reish= head. To speak is to bring an idea from the door in the head.

The Hebrew language has no word of "things," for "objects" or for "stuff: Even the words "physical" and "matter" are borrowed terms.

In Hebrew ALL THINGS ARE DVARIM – "WORDS!"

Words are articulations of the soul, crystallized thoughts. And ever since then, all that exists is God and His words.

The Structure Of The Letter Is Also Descriptive As To The Meaning Of A Word

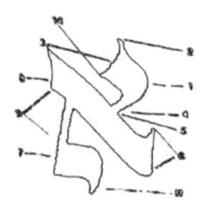

- Emet (Aleph, Mem, Tav) = **truth**. Each letter rests on two solid feet.

אמת

- Sheqer (Shin, Reish, Qof) = **false** (Lie), each letter is unstable on one point.

שרק

- While the Truth stands firmly, Lies have no feet, it looks good but rest on one point here one point there. One shove and it topples over.

Notes:_____

_____

_____

_____

_____

_____

_____

_____

_____

_____

_____

_____

_____

Emet also spans the entire alphabet with one the first letters at the beginning the second in the middle and the last letter at the end. From Aleph to Mem to Tav. Truth covers all points.

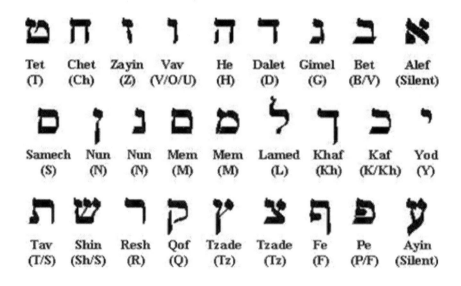

ט	ח	ז	ו	ה	ד	ג	ב	א
Tet	Chet	Zayin	Vav	He	Dalet	Gimel	Bet	Alef
(T)	(Ch)	(Z)	(V/O/U)	(H)	(D)	(G)	(B/V)	(Silent)

ס	ן	נ	ם	מ	ל	ך	כ	י
Samech	Nun	Nun	Mem	Mem	Lamed	Khaf	Kaf	Yod
(S)	(N)	(N)	(M)	(M)	(L)	(Kh)	(K/Kh)	(Y)

ת	ש	ר	ק	ץ	צ	ף	פ	ע
Tav	Shin	Resh	Qof	Tzade	Tzade	Fe	Pe	Ayin
(T/S)	(Sh/S)	(R)	(Q)	(Tz)	(Tz)	(F)	(P/F)	(Silent)

Sheqer = all letters are gathered together at the end. Falsehood only tells one side of the story.

1.3 WONDERFUL!

One of the things that proves God is God and false gods to be false is His mighty wonder working power.

In the Bible one of His attributes is described as omnipotent meaning God has all power.

A well-known Scripture from Exodus (or Shemot as the book is called in Hebrew) asks the question, "Who is like You, O LORD, among the gods? Who is like You, glorious in holiness, fearful in praises, doing wonders?" (Exod. 15:11), it is a beautiful description of God.

Exodus 15 includes the Song of Moses, sung immediately following the Children of Israel's miraculous deliverance at the crossing of the Red Sea. Truly they **must** have been overwhelmed by the greatness of God's power. How could anyone see the wonder-working power of God and His holy nature without recognizing Him as the King?

The word translated "wonders" is pele (פלה, pronounced with an "ph" sound rather than a hard "p" sound) and is found 13 times in Scripture. According to Strong's Concordance, it means a wonder, a miracle, and ***an extraordinary hard to understand thing.***

It comes from the root pala (same Hebrew letters but different vowel points), which means to be marvelous, wonderful, surpassing, extraordinary, and to be beyond one's power. This form of the word appears an additional 71 times in Scripture for a combined total of 84 times.

GIVE 3 WORDS TO DESCRIBE WONDERFUL THEN ACROSS FROM IT GIVE THE OPPOSITE OF THAT WORD.

1._____VS_____

2._____VS_____

3._____VS_____

In Genesis 18:14, pele is used to describe God's plan to bless Sarah and Abraham with a son: "Is [פלה] anything too hard [פלה] for the LORD? At the appointed time I will return to you, according to the time of life, and Sarah shall have a son."

As the Children of Israel were preparing to enter the Promised Land, God spoke to Joshua saying, "... Sanctify yourselves, for tomorrow the LORD will do wonders [פלה] among you" (Josh. 3:5).

Those who endure trials and who mourn find the book of Job to be a solace: "But as for me, I would seek God, and to God I would commit my cause—Who does great things, and unsearchable, marvelous things [פלה] without number" (Job 5:8–9).

In Isaiah 9, we have a beautiful description of the Messiah, "For unto us a Child is born, unto us a Son is given; and the government will be upon His shoulder. And His name will be called Wonderful [פלא], Counselor, Mighty God, Everlasting Father, Prince of Peace" (Isa. 9:6).

Notice, The Scripture does not say 'Wonderful Counselor' (although He is!), The Scripture says 'Wonderful' ,'Counselor' -2 separate attributes.

Wonder is one of those words that could be called a CONTRONYM meaning a word with opposite meanings.

- Examples of contronyms:

Cleave means to adhere or to separate.

First degree means the most sever in the case of a murder charge or least severe referring to a burn.

Trip means to take a journey or to stumble over something Wonder can be a hard to understand thing and a miracle. For this reason two distinct Hebrew words are used.

Pele is an **unusually hard to understand**.

A third word comes into play also "Oat" or "OT" meaning sign.

The basic nature of a sign is that it points people to God. "Wonders" describe God's supernatural activity, a special manifestation of His power (**Exodus 7:3**), but false prophets can perform actions people perceive as signs and wonders. (**Deuteronomy 13:1-3**). Wonders can serve as a sign of a future event. Signs seek to bring belief (**Exodus 4:5;** compare **Exodus 10:2**), but they do not compel a person to believe (**Exodus 4:9**). At times God invites people to ask for signs (**Isaiah 7:11**). The signs He has done should make all peoples on earth stand in awe.

(**Psalm 65:8**). They should join the Psalmist in confessing that the God of Israel "alone works wonders" (**Psalm 72:18).**

Notes:

THIS COURSE IS
CALLED *THE
'WONDERFUL
HEBREW ALPHABET*

BECAUSE BIBLICAL
HEBREW IS LASHON
HA KODESH, AN
UNUSUALLY HARD TO
UNDERSTAND THING
THAT IS BOTH A
MIRACLE AND A SIGN

CHAPTER 2

ALEPH THE LEADER

$\aleph$ = 1 or 1,000

First letter of the
Hebrew Alephbet.
It is silent.

2.1

Aleph is a silent letter. It has no sound. The sound it gets is from vowels
below, above or on the side of it. *The silence of Aleph should remind us that*

we are to approach God in reverence and in silence of His awesomeness before we begin to open our lips with praise or petitions.

"But Adonai is in His Holy temple; let all the earth be silent before him"- Habakuk 2:20 (CJB).

YAHSHUA (JESUS) IS THE WORD, THE BIBLE IS THE SCRIPTURES

JOHN 1:1-3 "IN THE BEGINNING WAS THE WORD AND THE WORD WAS WITH GOD AND THE WORD WAS GOD. HE WAS WITH GOD IN THE BEGINNING. ALL THINGS CAME TO BE THROUGH HIM AND WITHOUT HIM NOTHING MADE HAD BEING."

(CJB)

YAHSHUA (JESUS) SPOKE OF HIMSELF AS THE ALEPH TAV AND WAS SAYING THAT HE IS GOD'S ALPHABET. ALL COMMUNICATION IS THROUGH SPEECH OR JESTURES, ETC.

Hebrews 1 King James Version (KJV)

1   *God, who at sundry times and in divers manners spake in time past unto the fathers by the prophets,*

2   *Hath in these last days spoken unto us by his Son, whom he hath appointed heir of all things, by whom also he made the worlds;*

2.2

Aleph in Scriptures

As of the writing of the first version this workbook, Oct. 26, 2014 was Rosh Ha Shanna which literally means "head of the year", and is the New Year celebrating the creation of Adam. The year in 2014 was year 5,775 from creation. With the revision of the workbook in 2021, the year was 5781.

Yahshuah said " No man knows the day nor hour", of His return, only The Father in Heaven. However Yahweh graced us with times "oats"- signs to let us know when the time was approaching. The Feast Days (Holy Days) give us the clues. Yashuah was born during the Feast of Tabernacles. He "tabernacled" among us. He was crucified on Passover. The "Lamb of God". The Holy Spirit descended on Pentecost. There still remains Rosh Ha Shanna to be fulfilled.

Adam HaRishon was the name of the first ADAM. Yashuah Ha Maschiach is called the LAST ADAM.

The teaching that God has a 6,000year plan for the world before the Messiah returns is based on the fact that Aleph, which has a numerical value of 1 or 1,000 is present 6 times in the first sentence of the Bible. (See the circled letters below)

Also that there are six days of creation on which the Lord worked and the seventh day he hallowed, blessed and rested.

'For from your viewpoint a thousand years are merely like yesterday or a night watch' Psalm 90:4

"With the Lord a day is like a thousand years and a thousand years are like a day..." 2 Peter 3:8

God's name YAH = 15, the fifteenth letter from the beginning of the Bible again is Aleph.

Genesis Chapter 1 בְּרֵאשִׁית

א בְּרֵאשִׁית, בָּרָא אֱלֹהִים, אֵת הַשָּׁמַיִם, וְאֵת הָאָרֶץ.

1 In the beginning God created the heaven and the earth.

ב וְהָאָרֶץ, הָיְתָה תֹהוּ וָבֹהוּ, וְחֹשֶׁךְ, עַל-פְּנֵי תְהוֹם; וְרוּחַ אֱלֹהִים, מְרַחֶפֶת עַל-פְּנֵי הַמָּיִם.

2 Now the earth was unformed and void, and darkness was upon the face of the deep; and the spirit of God hovered over the face of the waters.

ג וַיֹּאמֶר אֱלֹהִים, יְהִי אוֹר; וַיְהִי-אוֹר.

3 And God said: 'Let there be light.' And there was light.

ד וַיַּרְא אֱלֹהִים אֶת-הָאוֹר, כִּי-טוֹב; וַיַּבְדֵּל אֱלֹהִים, בֵּין הָאוֹר וּבֵין הַחֹשֶׁךְ.

4 And God saw the light, that it was good; and God divided the light from the darkness.

ה וַיִּקְרָא אֱלֹהִים לָאוֹר יוֹם, וְלַחֹשֶׁךְ קָרָא לָיְלָה; וַיְהִי-עֶרֶב וַיְהִי-בֹקֶר, יוֹם אֶחָד. {פ}

5 And God called the light Day, and the darkness He called Night. And there was evening and there was morning, one day. {P}

(Psalm 68:4 ' Sing to God, sing praises to his name; extol him who rides on the clouds by His name, Yah; and be glad in his presence' (CJB) God's name El = 31, the 31st letter of the Bible is Aleph.

God's name Elohim =86, the 86th letter of the Bible is Aleph

AV (second letter of the alphabet is bet/vet)means father in Hebrew, the root of the word ABBA.

AV = 3, the 3rd letter of the Bible is Aleph.

Notes:_____

_____

_____

_____

_____

_____

It All Started With Adam!

אדם = ADAM

ALEPH - DALET- MEM

Adam is not just the name of the first man but God's name for "human being"".

Understanding the Hebrew word ADAM is the secret to understanding everything we are to be as a human being.

First of all it starts with the letter ALEPH which speaks of the Presence of God. We are made in the image of God and have the spark of God in us. Man's soul is described by Job as "a part of God above: Job 31:2. This divine spark is clothed with an earthly shell.

UNDER ADAM

Because of this, man can oscillate between crass hedonism and spiritual ecstasy. Before eating the forbidden fruit evil was external, enclothed with the Tree of Knowledge and the snake. Upon eating the forbidden fruit man internalized the struggle to determine between good and evil.

Next you have Dalet & Mem which spells Dam. Dam in Hebrew is BLOOD.

So we learn we have a Godly part, and we have a physical part.

But there's more here than just that. We can also see that our relationship with

God is a "Wonder!"

If we take the letter Aleph and write is out in English Aleph...but if we write it out in Hebrew we would write Aleph-Lamed-Peh. If we read that in the other direction...Peh-Lamed-Aleph we get the word Pela or Pele which is Wonder.

So this lets us know that our relationship with God always has an element of Wonder with it.

Let's look at something else.

More! Nothing else in creation can be MORE!. You can never expect a dog to be more of a dog, or a cat to be more of a cat, but you can expect a man to be more of a man. Or a woman to be more of a woman. That's because we were created with POTENTIAL! Just think of land. Why is it that land in one part of a city costs more than land in another part of the same town.

Isn't it all just land? The reason it costs more depends on the potential of what could be built on that land.

In ADAM we have the letters MEM-ALEPH-DALET which in Hebrew is Ma-ode meaning More, meaning we were created with POTENTIAL. We have the potential to be more. There are several names for man in the scriptures. Let's examine them.

Notes: _____

_____

_____

_____

_____

_____

The Bibles 4 words to describe man.

1. **ISH and ISHSHAH** (Man and Woman) in its' basic meaning means an individual.

Man wasn't called Ish in the scriptures until after Ishshah which is a man with a womb. There are times when the other words for "man" simply would not be appropriate. When the psalmist foretold that the names of those of the body of Christ who gain heavenly glory would be known, he could use only "ish" meaning each and every one was born in her.

1. **ADAM**- the human, the earthling. Adam is not a reference to man, but of a human being. Therefore, the scriptures state "Male and female created He them. And blessed them and called their name Adam." Genesis 5:2.

2. **ENOSH** - Mortal, weak and miserable.

3. **GEVER** – Able bodied, well developed, physically strong but inferior to his maker.

We should be reaching to be a Gever. We should be MORE than just a human being ruled by our animalistic nature.

Let's see what else we learn from the word ADAM.

Our Blood. We get our blood from our mothers and our fathers. From our AV and our AM. In Hebrew father is

אב = Aleph – Vav = AV where we get AVVA or ABBA.

אם = Mother = Aleph-Mem (pronounce Aim) If we take the numerical value of AV it's 1+2=3.

If we take the numerical value of AM it's 1+40= 41.

41+ 3 = 44! As Human beings we are 44. That's amazing when we understand that we have 44 chromosomes. 22 from our mother and 22 from our father. Before you get excited and say we have 46 chromosomes, let me explain.

We actually have 44 autosomes and 2 allosomes. Both are chromosomes. The allosomes are the sex chromosomes. Autosomes are labeled by numbers 1-22 depending on their size. So we have 22 Autosomes from our mother and 22 autosomes from our father. Allosomes are labeled by letters. So we have 1 allosome from our mother and 1 allosome from our father. 2 (x) allosomes determine a female and 1(x) and 1(y) determines a male. So the scriptures are correct in stating we have 44 chromosomes…not evolution which states we have 46 chromosomes because we have evolved! We have 44 chromosomes in number and 1 in letter….because at the core we are all 44!

Yet we are to aspire to be like 45.

We are called ADAM because we come from the ADAMAH, the earth. One of the meanings of the word Adamah means " I will resemble" We are to resemble the 45.

Where is the 45? Let's see!

Remember God's ineffable name? The Yod and Hei and Vav and Hei? There is the secret. Let's spell it out in Hebrew.

Yod = יוד =20

Hei = הא = 6

Vav = ויו = 13

Hei = הא = 6

20+ 6+ 13+6 = 45!

We are 44 but we are to resemble 45!

And all of this is hidden in God's word for human being "ADAM". Let's look at another secret hidden in the word ADAM.

What makes human beings different from animals? Well, so far we have seen a lot from studying the word ADAM. We are made in God's image, we have a spark of God within us, our relationship with God will always contain and element of Wonder, we are 44's that are to resemble the 45, but also the fact that we can be the controller instead of being controlled. When studying about blood and how the two letters in ADAM, the Dalet and the Mem spell DAM which means blood, there is another revelation. Many of our desires are in our blood and bloodline. Temperaments and passions usually originate there and are said to reside there. Being referred to as "Hot tempered" or "loss of control" has been associated with the blood. On a deeper level, the name ADAM alludes to man's ability to transcend these blood -born characteristics. In the next few paragraphs we will look at the characteristics of ALEPH. As a prelude, let's remember that ALEPH IS A CHIEF OR A GENERAL. A leader. Above, in front. And in the word ADAM, ALEPH IS BEFORE DAM, meaning that we can have control over the blood. ALEPH indicates leadership, as implied by the related word ALUF, WHICH MEANS A GENERAL OR A TRIBAL HEAD. While God created man with many desires that reside in the blood, He also gave us the means to assert our control over themand be an ALUF over the DAM. Be in control of, instead of subject to our base impulses, for we were created in the IMAGE OF GOD. Emulate Yahweh and work to be a 45!

ALEPH 3 IN ONE

Just as there are 3 parts to the Aleph that make on One letter and the number one, so there are 3 persons in the Godhead and 3 parts of a human being.

The Vav is the dominant part, representing the Father, the lower Yod representing YAHSHUA who came in earthly form and the upper Yod representing The Holy Spirit.

Likewise, in humans, the greatest of God's creation, made in the image of God, there is the dominant part, represented by the vav is the soul where our mind, will and emotions reside. then the lower Yod representing the body, Yod is also a picture of a hand and just as the hand has 5 fingers, the body has 5 senses

…seeing, hearing, smelling, touching, tasting. The upper Yod represents the spirit of man which also has five spiritual senses....faith, conscience, discernment, communication, and worship.

Notes:_____

_____

_____

_____

_____

_____

_____

2.4

THE CHARACTERISTICS OF ALEPH

Aleph as a Picture

The pictorial image for ALEPH is an **OX** representing the characteristics of strength, power and chief.

Adam (spelled Aleph Dalet final Mem) shows man is created in the image of God.

The Aleph represents God's presence. If the Aleph is removed we are left with the word Dam which means 'blood'. And so it is when we ignore the image and presence of God in another human being it results in bloodshed.

ALEPH AS A LEADER LETTER

- First letter of the Hebrew Alphabet.

- First letter of many of God's names.

- Considered a Holy letter.

- Aleph is not the first letter of the Torah, but it we start with the first letter which is a Beit and count 26 letters we come to letter Aleph.

ALEPH AS A NUMBER

Aleph is the number 1 (or 1,000)

- THE TOTAL NUMERICAL VALUE is 26 WHICH IS THE NUMERICAL VALUE OF THE 4 LETTER NAME OF GOD YHVH.

- KNOWN AS THE TETRAGRAMMATON (GREEK MEANING "FOUR

LETTERS").

- YOD = 10, HEI = 5, VAV = 6, Hei = 5 TOTAL 26.

- YHVH IS GOD'S NAME THAT WAS FIRST REVEALED TO MOSES WHEN GOD SENT HIM TO DELIVER THE ISRAELITES FROM EGYPTIAN BONDAGE.

Exodus 3:13 "MOSHE SAID TO GOD" LOOK, WHEN I APPEAR BEFORE THE PEOPLE OF ISRA'EL AND SAY TO THEM ' THE GOD OF YOUR ANCESTORES HAS SENT ME TO YOU' ; AND THEY ASK ME ' WHAT IS HIS NAME/ WHAT AM I TO TELL THEM?

EXODUS 3:14 GOD SAID TO MOSHE

E'hyeh Asher   E'hyeh

I AM/WILL BE   WHAT   I AM/ WILL BE

Exodus 3:15 reads:

"GOD SAID FURTHER TO MOSHE, "SAY THIS TO THE PEOPLE OF Isra'el'; ' YUD-HEH-VAV-HEH (ADONAI) THE GOD OF YOUR FATHERS, THE GOD OF AVRAHAM, THE GOD OF YITZ'CHAK AND THE GOD OF YAA'AKOV, HAS SENT ME TO YOU, THIS IS MY NAME FOREVER, THIS IS HOW I AM TO BE REMEMBERED GENERATION AFTER GENERATION"- CJB

YHVH - THE INEFFABLE NAME OF GOD. **TOO GREAT TO BE UTTERRED!**

THIS HOLY NAME OF GOD IS NOT PRONOUNCED BECAUSE WE DON'T

KNOW THE PROPER PRONUNCIATION. THE KJV AND BIBLE TRANSLATORS TRANSLATE THIS NAME AS LORD, JEHOVAH, OR ADONAI, BUT THE PRONUNCIATION WAS ONLY HANDED DOWN VERBALLY FOR GENERATIONS AND HAS BEEN LOST THROUGH TIME.

THIS NAME WAS PRONOUNCED IN THE HOLY OF HOLIES BY THE HIGH PRIEST ONCE PER YEAR.

BECAUSE OF ITS GREATNESS WE DARE NOT ATTEMPT TO TRANSLATE IT IN ERROR.

THIS NAME CAN NEVER BE ERASED WHEN WRITTEN BY A SCRIBE. IT IS CALLED THE INEFFABLE NAME OF GOD. (TOO GREAT OR EXTREME TO BE EXPRESSED OR DESCRIBED IN WORDS)

BEFORE THE NAME IS WRITTEN THE SCRIBE ANNOUNCES HE IS PREPARING TO WRITE THE NAME OF GOD IN HONOR OF HIS HOLY NAME. HE CAN NOT BE INTERRUPTED BY ANYONE OR ANYTHING WHEN WRITING THE NAME OF GOD.

MANY TIMES IN AN EFFORT TO AVOID TAKING GOD'S NAME IN VAIN AND REVERENCE FOR THE 4 LETTER NAME OF GOD MANY OBSERVANT BELEIVERS WILL STATE IT AS YOD AND HEI VAV AND HEI AS NOT TO SAY ALL 4 LETTERS TOGETHER.

ALEPH- AS THE TORAH

JOHN 3:17 "FOR GOD DID NOT SEND THE SON INTO THE WORLD TO JUDGE THE WORLD, BUT RATHER SO THAT THROUGH HIM THE WORLD MIGHT BE SAVED" - CJB

- **YOD** IS THE SYMBOL FOR HAND.

- **VAV** IS THE SYMBOL FOR MAN.

The construction of the Aleph shows an upper hand which is understood as the hand of God reaching down and the lower hand which is understood as the hand of man reaching up and the slanted vav as the Messiah YAHSHUAh who as the living word put on human flesh and humbled himself even to death on a tree to be the one mediator between God and man.

1 Timothy 2:5 .

"For God is one; and there is but one Mediator between God and humanity. YAHSHUA the Messiah, himself human…" – **CJB**

X X X X X

_____

_____

_____

_____

_____

CHAPTER 3

BEIT   THE   HOUSE

3.1

Bet/vet

BEIT ב

ב = 2   Beit is the second letter of the Hebrew Alphabet and the first

letter of The Bible.

"Bet" (rhymes with "mate") and has the sound of "b" as in"boy.

- First Letter of Bible is an oversized Beit and the **only** oversized Beit in the Bible.

- Name meaning = House = ב'ת.

- Bethel " House of God", Bethlehem " House of Bread."

- Beit is the dwelling place for the YAHSHUA, The Word and for mankind The Scriptures are literally "writings" ... ink on paper.

YAHSHUA is The Living Word.

The Words that He spoke/ speaks are Spiritual and Alive.

"It is the spirit that quickens; the flesh profits nothing; the words that I speak to you, they are spirit and they are life. " - John 6:63.

YAHSHUA was The Word that was in the Beginning.

3.2

Beit as a house   בר אשית

בראשית

654321

The letters in the middle of the word, Reish, Aleph, and Shin spell the word "Rosh" Which means Head. Rosh Chodesh means Head of the month. Head in the middle of this word speaks of "The Head of the House" YAHSHUA is the head of the house. ר

He is actually present in the word Beginning "Barasheit".

In the BEGINNING was THE WORD! – John 1:1-2….and the WORD was WITH

GOD, and THE WORD WAS GOD...THE SAME WAS IN THE BEGINNING with God

The second "house" that Barasheit speaks of is The Temple of which it is

written in the scriptures "My house will be called a house of prayer for all people."

Isaiah 56:7 & Matthew 21:13.

BET is the Hebrew word for HOUSE and for TEMPLE.

Yahshua DIVIDED Himself from His Father's HOUSE in Heaven to come to earth and UNITE with mankind. Yahshua came to Tabernacle with us.

Yahshua explained, "Destroy this TEMPLE, and in 3 days I will raise it up…But He spoke of the TEMPLE of His Body." (John 2:19 & 21) Messiah IS our Home…

We abide in Him. And He desires to make His Home (TEMPLE) in our hearts.

Next there is the house of creation. The Hebrew alphabet is the building blocks for creation. God spoke the universe into creation. The Aleph is silent and from the next letter, the Beit is the house out of which all the letters of creation came. Beit is always printed in Torah scrolls with two sharp points.

A Jewish story explains these two points: If you should ask the beith " Who made you?", it points up toward God. If you ask it "What is His name?" it points backward toward the aleph.

3.3

BEIT AS THE SHEEPFOLD GATE.

John 10:1 " Verily, verily I say unto you , he that enters by the door of the sheepfold, but climbs up some other way is a thief and a robber.

One mathematical arrangement of the letter **rosh is osher**, **"happiness."** When the *righteous person* draws God, the "Head," into His House, it becomes a house of true and eternal happiness.

Also in the word **Bara,** which is also the second word of the Bible. **Bara** means **"Created"** Bara is only possible through God because Bara is to make something out of nothing.

Barasheit bara Elohim et HaShamyaim v' et eretz.

In the Beginning of God's Creating God created the heaven and earth

….All things were Created by Him (The Word) and without Him was nothing made that was created" - John 1:3.

Beth-El Yahshua is said to have "tabernacled" with us (John 1:14), Whose Body was indeed (Bet-El), the habitation of God Almighty.

bara ברא☺"Create" – Bara is always applied to Yahweh's.

Ability to Create, never man's, because it means to form something out of nothing, which only God can do. Starting the "Create" Word with BEIT shows that Creation without YAH Tabernacling (being Present) in the process is impossible.

bana בנא☺Bana means to "build". Bana is something mankind can do, yet the presence of the BEiT, as the first letter, shows YAH Tabernacling within, enabling the building. "Unless Yahweh build the house, they labor in vain that build it…"

Yahshua is proclaimed by both BARA and BANA, as the Great Architect and Builder.

The Hebrew word for "son" is "BEN". But BAR, the Aramaic word for son, is also frequently used in the Bible. By simply distancing the aleph from the first two letters of ברא☉ (BARA) and בכא☉ (BANA), we get: א (Son (of = א bar א

בר☉ create."

We can see in BARA and BANA, two outstanding attributes of Yahshua, the Great Creator and Builder. Abraham may have been aware of these Truths.… "For he was looking forward to the City with Foundations, Whose Architect and Builder is God." In Genesis 1:1, the first word is (barasheit, "in the beginning"), and the second word is ברא☉ (bara, "create.

Notes:_____

_____

_____

_____

_____

_____

_____

_____

_____

_____

_____

_____

BEIT is the number of DIVISION and of UNITY. Yahshua is the Great Divider. He is our Righteous Judge Who will come in His Glory. "And before Him shall be gathered all nations; and He shall separate them one from another, as a shepherd DIVIDES his sheep from the goats,"

Beit has the basic gematria number of 2

- Dualistic nature of creation.

- Divine power of Self to contain two opposites.

The gematria of beit is two. Two represents duality and plurality. Everything in Creation was created in pairs. Man and woman, male and female. This reminds us that we are not GOD. Only GOD can be One. But for mankind to create, to reproduce, two are required. Beit also represents the level of intellect, in contrast to the alef, which represents faith.

The commentaries on the Torah ask, "Why does the Torah begin with the letter beit instead of an alef?" particularly when the Zohar states that the alef is the holiest letter (because it is first in the order of the alef-beit).

The Rebbe gives the following explanation: When a person reads the beginning of the Torah, he wonders: "Why does the Torah begin with a beit, the second letter of the alef-beit? Why doesn't the Torah begin with the first letter, the alef?" And the answer unfolds as follows:

In Jeremiah the question is asked: "Why was the land of Israel destroyed?" GOD answers, "Because the Jewish people have forsaken My Torah." The Talmud counters, "What do you mean they didn't learn Torah? [The Jewish people were constantly studying Torah.]" The Talmud thus deduces that the reason the land was destroyed was that the Jews didn't make a blessing before they began to study the Torah.

What is the blessing over the Torah? "Blessed are You, GOD our LORD, King of the universe, Who has chosen us out of all nations of the world, and given us His Torah [(i.e., not a man-made Torah, but dictated by GOD to Moses letter by letter; and as such, true and unchanged for all generations)], blessed are You GOD Who gives the Torah."

A person must verbalize this introductory blessing every day before he begins to study Torah. Rabbi Yoel Sirkis explains that the purpose of Torah study is to "cleave and become one with GOD through the holiness of His word, and thereby cause the *Shechinah*, the Divine Presence of GOD, to dwell amongst us." Indeed, there are two levels to our relationship with the Torah. The first is to believe with complete faith that the Torah comes from GOD (and is therefore beyond human intellect); and the second, that it is only because of GOD's compassion and love for His people that He allows us to understand the Torah intellectually.

If one denies the divinity of Torah, one cannot properly understand its Godly concepts. Our intellect alone is incapable of arriving at the true meaning of the Torah's contents. - Rabbi Aaron L. Raskin.

Construction Form = 3 VAVs open on left side.

- The House is a roof on top a wall on the right side and a floor on the bottom representing **what is above, below or came before is hidden.**

- 3 VAVs = 18 the number for Chai (Life)

- The three lines of the *beit* are often interpreted as representing the three pillars on which the world stands: Torah, prayer, and charity (including good deeds).

When a person prays,

studies Torah, and gives

charity daily, one builds a

home for God.

בבבבב

_____

_____

_____

_____

CHAPTER 4

The Greatest of these is CHARITY

ג=3

4.1

GIMMEL THE RICH MAN/DALET THE POOR

GIMMEL / DALET

Because of their union Gimmel and Dalet must be taught together.

GIMMEL AS THE RICH MAN

Our Sages teach that the *gimel* symbolizes a rich man running after a poor man, the *dalet*, to give him charity. The word "*gimel*" is derived from the word "*gemul*", which in Hebrew means both the giving of reward as well as the giving of punishment. In Torah, both reward and punishment have the same ultimate aim: the rectification of the soul to merit to receive GOD's light to the fullest extent.

Reward and punishment imply that man is free to choose between good and evil.

- the leg of the letter *gimel* which expresses the running of the rich man to bestow good upon the poor man.

- Running, more than any other physical act, expresses the power of will and freedom of choice (the Hebrew word for "running", "*ratz*", is related to the word for "will","*ratzon*").

- In running, the leg is firmly in contact with the earth; through an act of will, the soul directly affects physical reality.

Gimmel   גמל   Dalet   דלת

Gimmel – Mem- Lamed   Dalet –Lamed- Tav

4.2

PROHIBITION AGAINST DELAY

The ultimate definition of "poor" is Lamed which means poor in knowledge. Those that are Gamul in knowledge should teach those that are poor in knowing.

Deut. 15:7-11 … For the poor shall never cease out of the land…."

Matt 26:6 -11 ".For you have the poor with you always…"

The Talmud states **THERE ARE ALWAYS POOR PEOPLE NEEDING IMMEDIATE HELP.**

In the case of charity it must be given

immediately, for the poor are always to

be found –

Tractate Rosh HaShanna Chapter 1

4.3

CHARACTERISTICS OF GIMMEL

Picture: Camel and **Forerunner**

FORM: A *vav* with a *yud* as a foot. A person in motion.

Number: 3 **(Total sum of Aleph + Beit = Gimmel)**

3's in the Bible.

3 divisions of the Bible: Torah, The Prophets,and the Writings.

3 Pillars on which the world stands, Torah, Prayer (sacrifice) and Charity.

- 3 Fathers: Abraham, Isaac, and Jacob.

- 3 divisions of Jewish souls: kohanim (priests), Leviim (levites), and Israelites.

- 3 persons used to bring the Israelites out of Egyptian bondage: Moses, Aaron and Mariam.

- 3 Sections of the Temple: The Outer court, the Inner Court and the Holy of Holies.

- 3 Major Holy Days we MUST appear before the Lord, Passover, Pentecost, and Feast of Tabernacles.

- 3 that bear witness in Heaven, The Father, the Word and The Holy Ghost.

- 3 that bear witness on Earth, The Spirit, the Blood and the Water.

- 3 disciples in YAHSHUA's inner circle: Peter, James and John.

- 3 abide, Faith, Hope and Charity....these three, and the greatest of these is Charity.

- 3 Divisions of Time, Past, present and future.

- 3 involved in the creation of a child, Mother, Father and God.

- 3 parts of man, Soul, Spirit, and Body.

- 3 times the angel cry "holy, holy, holy" in heaven.

- 3 Primary elements of Creation, Air, Fire, and Water.

- Earth is the 3rd Planet from the sun.

4.4

GIMMEL AS THE FORERUNNER

The Aleph represents Yahweh, The Beit represents Yahshua, who tabernacle among us and the Gimmel represents The Holy Spirit as He was manifested in John the Baptist, the forerunner of the Messiah.

7   And as they departed, Jesus began to say unto the multitudes concerning John, What went ye out into the wilderness to see? A reed shaken with the wind?

8   But what went ye out for to see? A man clothed in soft raiment? behold, they that wear soft clothing are in kings' houses.

9   But what went ye out for to see? A prophet? yea, I say unto you, and more than a prophet.

10   For this is he, of whom it is written, Behold, I send my messenger before thy face, which shall prepare thy way before thee.

11   Verily I say unto you, Among them that are born of women there hath not risen a greater than John the Baptist: notwithstanding he that is least in the kingdom of heaven is greater than he.

–Matt 11:7-11

Gimel

is said to represent a man

with head bent, determined to

travel from the second letter

(beit) to the fourth letter (dalet)

The Gimmel is the forerunner of the

Beit (Yashua). This secret is revealed

in the clothes worn by John the Baptist.

Gimmel also represents camel and we

are told in the scriptures that John the

Baptist was in the wilderness and his

clothes were made of camel hair. The

word for garment is beged, spelled

(Beit, Gimmel, Dalet). These are the

second, third and fourth letter of the

Hebrew alphabet. In other words

gimmel represents a man dressed up

like a camel coming out of the house

and is on an important mission to

the Dalet, the poor.

Now we can see why John said he that comes AFTER me but is preferred BEFORE me.

Another point about John the Baptist is his diet was locusts and honey. The second and third letter of the alphabet (gimmel, vet) spells Gav which means locust.

4.5

GIMMEL AS THE HOLY SPIRIT

Gimmel represents the number 3, and the Holy Spirit comes to convict the world of three things.

When He comes, He will convict the world of:

1. Sin, because Men do not believe in Me.

2. Of Righteousness because I am going to the Father.

3. Of Judgement because the prince of this world now stands condemned.

Notes:_____

_____

_____

_____

_____

_____

ג ג ג ג ג

_____

_____

DALET THE POOR MAN

The dalet. the poor man, receives charity from the rich man, the gimel. The word dalet means "door." The door stands in the opening of the house, the beit.

- the *dalet* characterizes "shiflut," "lowliness," the consciousness of possessing nothing of one's own.

- Together with the awareness of one's own power of free choice, one must be aware that He gives you the power to achieve success, and not to think, God forbid, that one's accomplishments are "my power and the strength of my hand." Any achievement in this world, particularly the performance of a *mitzvah*, (commandment) the fulfillment of God's will, depends upon Divine aid.

- one's struggle with his evil inclination, whether it be manifest as external passion, stubborn resistance to accepting the yoke of Heaven, or laziness, apathy, and the like. As our Sages teach: "If not for God's help he [man] would not have been able to overcome it [the evil inclination]."

- Free choice is no more than the expression of one's will to participate, For to You,

"For to You, God, is kindness, for You pay man in accordance with his deed."

- Just payment in accordance with one's deed is not an act of kindness (*chesed*), but rather one of judgment (*din*)!

- Thus God's ultimate kindness is His clothing the "undeserved" reward in the guise of deservedness, so as not to shame the receiver.

- *chesed* as *chas d'leit*, "having compassion [on] the *dalet*," i.e. he who possesses nothing of his own.

4.7

CHARACTERISTICS OF DALET

PICTURE:

 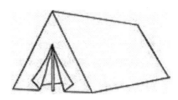

Tent door

FORM: The first line on top goes past the vertical line on the bottom.

NAME Door; path , entrance, poor man;

- Door–*bitul*, the entrance way to truth.

- A door also separates.

- The servant who refuses to go through the door of freedom.

- Derrek = the way.

- Debber = go back to the source of food.

- Debar= pestilence.

NUMBER FOUR

- Four elements of the physical world: fire, air, water, and earth.

- Solid, liquid, gas, combustion.

- Hydrogen, carbon, nitrogen, oxygen.

- The four physical forces: gravity, electromagnetic, strong, weak.

- Man, animal, vegetable, and inanimate objects.

- Four seasons of the year; Four directions.

- Four matriarchs: Sarah, Rebecca, Rachel, and Leah.

- Jacob's four wives: Rachel, Leah, Bilhah, and Zilpah.

- The four cups of wine of the *Seder.*

- Cup of Sanctification "I will bring you out of Egypt.

- Cup of Deliverance "I will deliver you from Egyptian slavery."

- Cup of Redemption "I will redeem you with My power."

- Cup of Restoration : I will take you as My people."

- Father, mother, son, daughter: the first commandment of the Torah:

- "be fruitful and multiply."

- 4 Kingdoms to rule: Babylon, Persia, Greece, Rome.

- 4 horsemen of the apocalypse Divinity:

- Four letters of God's Name.

- Four basic levels of Torah interpretation. (PaRDeS)

- Parshat

- Remez

- Drash

- Sod

T T T T T

CHAPTER 5

THE WINDOW

אב גדה

ה = 5

BEHOLD!

Hel   ה

5.1

THE UNIQUINESS OF THE HEI

- 50% OF THE FOUR LETTER NAME OF GOD.

- THE HEI ALONE CAN STAND FOR THE NAME OF GOD.

Creation begins with Adam but

JUDAISM BEGINS WITH ABRAM WHEN HE BECAME A JEW GOD CHANGED HIS NAME TO ABRA-HAM) AV HA MON GOYIM) FATHER OF MANY NATIONS SARAI GOD CHANGED HER NAME TO SARAH.

SARAI MEANS MY PRINCESS- SARAH MEANS PRINCESS IN THE ACCOUNT OF THE CREATION OF THE WORLD GENESIS 2:4 THE HEI IS WRITTEN DIFFERENT, IT IS SMALLER.

בהבראם (WITH THE HEI HE CREATED THEM. GOD CREATED THE WORLD WITH A HEI).

PSALM 33:6 "By the word of the LORD were the heavens made; and all the host of them by the breath of his mouth."

- TESHUVAH - RETURN THE HEI

- "Where are you in reference to the Hei

- Hei and Tehsuvah. Since the Hey is formed of Dalet and Yod it can also be a picture of returning to God by means of the transforming power of the Spirit. Dalet stands for brokenness and Yod stands for a hand.

Grain and Seed

Grain is to be **revealed** and seed is to be **concealed**

Hei appears in the verse "Take (hei) for yourselves seed" "Take (hei) expresses concealment of self in the act of giving of oneself to another.

Highest forms of charity is giving where the giver is concealed. In the Hei the gift is the expression of self.

8 LEVELS OF CHARITY

(From highest to lowest)

8. The greatest level is to support a fellow brother or sister by strengthening his/her hand until he is no longer dependent on others. Ie. Finding employment, giving a business loan, entering into partnership.

7. To give to the poor without either party knowing who gave or who received.

6. To give when the giver knows who the recipient is but the receiver doesn't know who gave.

5. When the receiver knows who gave but the giver doesn't know who he gave to.

4. To give directly in hand but before being asked.

3. To give after being asked.

2. To give inadequately but give gladly and with a smile.

1. And the lesser level of giving is to give unwillingly.

5.3

THE HEI IN MARRIAGE

The *Talmud*[7] tells us that if man and woman, איש ואשה (*ish v'isha*), are meritorious, the Divine presence will rest between them.

The word *ish*, man, is spelled איש, *alef, yud, shin. Isha*, אשה, woman, is spelled *alef, shin, hei*.

In both *ish* and *isha* we find the letters *alef* and *shin*. *Alef* and *shin* spell *eish*, the Hebrew word for fire. The fire that exists between man and woman fuels a fiery, passionate relationship. But if there were *only* this flame igniting the marriage, the fire of passion could all too easily be transformed into a fire of destruction. God must also be in the marriage, and fortunately He is: the *yud* of the *ish*, the man, when combined with the *hei* of the *isha*, the woman, denotes the very name of God.

The comparison of a husband and wife's relationship to fire illustrates the secret to a healthy marriage. When two people decide to marry, there is usually fire and passion. Yet for some reason, two or three years down the line, the excitement is often gone. No fire. Where did the passion go?

5.4

CHARACTERISTICS OF THE HEI

Name: Hei = to be broken, to take seed, behold, revelation.

Form

Three lines= 3 garments of expression

- *Thought*

- *Speech*

- *Action*

Number Hei = 5

- *5 senses*

- *5 fingers*

- *5 toes*

- *5 books of Moses*

5 levels of the soul

a. *Nefesh= Instincts of the Soul*

b. *Ruach= Emotions of the Soul*

c. *Nashamah= Intellect of the Soul*

d. *Chaya = Bridge to transcendence*

e. *Yechida= Oneness*

Picture Hei = WINDOW or A MAN RAISING HIS HANDS

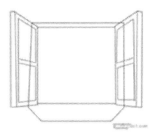

BEHOLD

NOTES:

CHAPTER 6

VAV = MAN

א ב ג ד ה ו

ו= 6

6.1

VAV OR WAW ו

The SIXTH LETTER OF THE HEBREW ALPHABET VAV represents " AND" The first VaV in the scriptures is in Genesis 1:1.

It is the first letter of the 6th word and the 22nd letter of the scriptures.

In the beginning God created the heaven and the earth.

It connects HaShamiyam (Heaven) with Eretz (earth)" and" being so it points to the creative connection of all the 22 letters of the Hebrew Alphabet.

The Vav IS A REMINDER of the connection between spiritual world and the earthly world.

THE VAV AS A HOOK

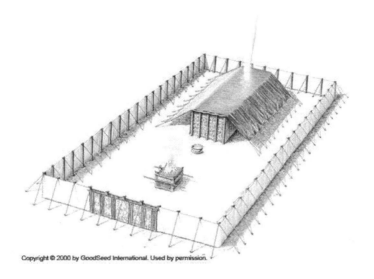

Copyright © 2000 by GoodSeed International. Used by permission.

In Exodus 27: 9-10 the word VaV is used to refer to the silver hooks that fastened to the posts that held the curtain that surrounded the tabernacle.

The tabernacle was the habitation of God and the Torah is the habitation of His Word so The Torah is constructed in the likeness of the Tabernacle. The Torah must not have any errors whatsoever and each line is written according to over 4,000 laws. The lines are carefully read backwards and if any errors are discovered the Torah is considered invalid and the parchment must be removed and buried in a cemetery for sacred texts.

- The posts are called AMUDIM.

- The curtain is called YERIAH.

- There are 304,805 letters in the Torah Scroll.

- The parchment pages of the scroll are called YERIAH just as the curtain in the tabernacle.

- Each Parchment must come from the hide of a Kosher animal that has been specially prepared for the purpose of writing.

- Special inks are used.

- Every time a scribe writes one of the 7 names of God, he must say a blessing and dip his quill in fresh ink.

- There are approximately 50 Yeriot per Torah Scroll.

- The column in the Torah scroll are called AMUD just as the posts of the Tabernacle.

- There are 248 AMUD per Torah scroll.

- Each column begins with the letter Vav, to hook the words to the parchment.

6.3

THE VAV'S EFFECT ON TIME

In Biblical Hebrew, the letter vav also possesses the function of inverting the apparent tense of a verb to its opposite from past to future or from future to past (vav hahipuch).

The first appearance of this type of vav in the Torah is the letter vav" which begins the twenty second word of the

The power of Teshuvah to completely convert ones past to good is the power of the vav to invert the past to the future.

In the divine service of a Jew, the power to draw from the future into the past is the secret of Teshuvah ('repentance' and 'returning to God') from love.

Through Teshuvah from fear, one's deliberate transgressions become like errors, the severity of one's past transgressions becomes partially sweetened, but not completely changed. However when a Jew returns in love, his deliberate transgressions become like actual merits for the very consciousness of distance from God resulting from one's transgressions becomes the motivating force to return to God with passion even greater than that of one who had never sinned.

The phenomenon of light breaking through the darkness of the tzimtzum, the primordial contraction, is itself the secret of time (future becoming past) which permeates space.

In the Divine service of a Jew, the power to draw from the future into the past is the secret of teshuvah ("repentance" and "returning to God") from love.

Through teshuvah from fear, one's deliberate transgressions become like errors; the severity of one's past transgressions becomes partially sweetened, but not completely changed. However, when a Jew returns in love, his deliberate transgressions become like actual merits, for the very consciousness of distance from God resulting from one's transgressions becomes the motivating force to return to God with passion even greater than that of one who had never sinned.

The power of teshuvah to completely convert one's past to good, is the power of the vav to invert the past to the future.

Every Jew has a portion in the World to Come, as is said: "And all your nation are 'tzadikim'; forever they will inherit the land.") Isaiah 60:21.

The power of teshuvah to completely convert one's past to good, is the power of the vav to invert the past to the future. This transformation itself requires, paradoxically, the drawing down of light from the future to the past. Drawing the future into the past in the Divine service of man is the secret of learning the inner teachings of the Torah, that aspect of the Torah which is related to the revelation of the coming of the Mashiach.

CHARACTERISTICS OF VAV

FORM:

A vertical line.

A pillar.

Used as a vowel. When you put a dot over it is produces an 'O' sound. When you put a dot to the left (Inside of it) it produces a 'U' sound.

The Word of God became flesh and was nailed to a tree. The Aleph-Tav **א– ת** which is all the letters of the Hebrew alphabet (Word) when a vav is put in the middle now means "a sign" as in " I am only going to give you one sign, the sign of Jonah…" So with the vav as a nail, you are nailing the Word of God to a tree - Hidden truth revealed.

Picture

VAV= Hook, or a nail, to join, to pierce, also means "and" to connect two things together or A man standing upright.

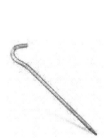 

NUMBER:SiX

Six Days of Creation, and their six corresponding Divine forces active in creation. Six letters of the word bereishit, "In the beginning." Six alefs in the first verse of the Torah.

Six-millennium duration of the world.

Six directions of the physical world. North , South, East, West, Up, Down

Man was created on the Sixth day/ The Beast was created on the Sixth Day Man works for Six days.

The beast is identified as the 'number of a man" 666

Actually the number is not 666 but Six hundred and Sixty Six.

CHAPTER 7

ZAYIN = SWORD

אב גדהוז

ז= 7

THE SWORD & CROWN

ZAYIN

The seventh letter of the Hebrew Alphabet looks like a sword but comes from a root word meaning "nourishment" The word "zan" is in the word 'mazon' = food.

The letter zayin is a paradox. On one end it means sword, relative to war on the other end food or nourishment.

The word for bread 'lechem' is in the Hebrew word' for war 'milchamah.

לחם

מלחמה

Not war and fighting for greed but sometimes we must fight to protect our lives and our way of life.

THE WOMAN OF VALOR — PROVERBS 31

Zayin also means crown.

The *Maggid of Mezeritch*, the successor of the *Ba'al Shem Tov*, teaches that the verse "A woman of valor is the crown of her husband" alludes to the form of the letter *zayin*. The previous letter, *vav*, portrays the *or yashar* ("straight light") descending from God into the worlds. The *zayin*, whose form is similar to a *vav*, but with a crown on top, reflects the *or yashar* of the *vav* as *or chozer* ("returning light"). The straight light as the returning light.

The experience of *or chozer*, the creation of man on the sixth day, is the secret of the seventh day of Creation–*Shabbat*.

The *Shabbat* Queen" who, in general, signifies woman in relation to man–"the woman of valor is the crown of her husband"– has the power to reveal in her husband his own superconscious crown, the experience of serene pleasure and sublime will that is realized in the day of *Shabbat*.

"Who is a good [literally, "kosher"] woman? She who does her husband's will." the word "does" also means "rectifies," She helps to put it right and correct it.

Thus the "kosher woman" is she who rectifies her husband's will by elevating him to ever new awareness of superconscious realms of soul. (Moving into another level of understanding who he is in God).

7.2

ACROSTICS IN THE HEBREW BIBLE

One of the many interesting rhetorical features of the Hebrew Bible is its use of alphabetical acrostics. These acrostics are not "hidden codes" -- they are literary compositions in which the writer has used the <u>letters of the Hebrew alphabet</u> as the initial letters for a sequence of verses. This feature is described as "a poetic way of saying that a total coverage of the subject was being offered."

In the common form of acrostic found in Old Testament Poetry, each line or stanza begins with a letter of the Hebrew alphabet in order. This literary form may have been intended as an aid to memory, but more likely it was a poetic way of saying that a total coverage of the subject was being offered -- as we would say 'from A to Z.

7.3

THE SWORD OF ZAYIN

The sword mentioned in Hebrews 4:12 is the Greek word "machaira' meaning a 'short sword' that was sharpened on both edges of the blade. The two edges represent the two main parts of the scriptures (The old and new testaments).

The Zayin is used to cut up time into increments of seven.

- Shabbat – the 7th day.

- Shavu'ot – the 49th day after Passover.

- Tishri- The seventh month.

- Shemitah – the 7th year of rest for the land

- Yovel- the 49th year.

- The Millennial Kingdom – the 7th millennium of human history.

- The sanctity of seven is not only true in the microcosm, but in the macrocosm as well. With the First Day of Creation representing the first thousand years of the world's existence, the Second Day representing the second thousand years, etc., Shabbos represents the Seventh Millennium, which is "a day of rest and tranquility for all eternity."

- One of the things that tempt us during the work-week is our belief that it is our ability and efforts alone that shape and control our fate. This belief then opens the door to the evil inclination in all its facets. The crown and sword of Shabbos remind us that.

- GOD and only GOD is the Master of our fate, and this belief gives us the ability to conquer all negative forces. Indeed, blessings are our truest, most reliable weapons.

- This is the secular year 2014- 2015 As we are currently in the year 5775 from Creation, we are now in the Sixth Millennium. To figure out what "time" we're inhabiting in that millennium, we need to make some calculations: One thousand years represents one day, or 24 hours of creation. One thousand divided by 24 is 41.67 years per universal hour. If we then divide 41.67 into 775 (the years left after removing the root 5,000, signifying the Sixth Millennium) we get 18.60. We are thus currently 18.60 hours (approximately 18 hours and 60 minutes) past the preceding sunset, and are in "Friday afternoon," aprox. 4:30 pm at the cusp of Shabbos. We are living right on the edge of the Seventh Millennium, the eternal Shabbos, the "day" of eternal tranquility. And when do we begin preparing in earnest for Shabbos as well as for *Mashiach's* arrival? Whether by the clock or calendar, it's Friday at noon (12:00 noon/the year 5750)! Preparation for this era is not something we can scramble for at the very last minute. It is something we must build toward with intention and joy.

ZAYIN IS NOT PRESENT IN PSALM 91

- Even though it is a warfare Psalm. Demons are mentioned by name in that Psalm.

"Sha'atnez gets" letters

- Eight Hebrew letters are given special adornment by attaching three "tagin" or crownlets to them called sha'atnezgets letters. Some of the sages have said that these crownlets are actually small "zaynin" so that, for example, when Psalm 91 is recited, they function as spiritual weapons.

- The name zayin means "crown." There are actually crowns, called zayenin, on many of the letters of the alef-beit.

- DEVER ("Pestilence") is the other demonic herald who marches with with YHWH to battle (Hab. 3:5). Dever is also mentioned in Psalms 91:5–6 "Thou shalt not be afraid for the Terror (*Paḥad*) by night; Nor for the Arrow (*Ḥez*) that flieth by day; Nor for the Pestilence (*Dever*) that walketh in the darkness; Nor for the Destruction (*Ketev*) that wasteth at noonday." Not only Dever but also the other words italicized above have been plausibly identified as names of demons. The "Arrow" is a familiar symbol in folklore, for disease or sudden pain, and *Ketev* (*Qetev*; cf. Deut. 32:24; Isa. 28:2; Hos. 13:14) is in this instance the personification of overpowering noonday heat, known also to Greek and Roman demonology.

Words that begin with Zayin:

- Zman = Time

- Zicharon = rememberance

- The oversized Zayin is found in Malachi 4:4

"Remember the Torah of Moses my servant that I commanded him at Horeb, the statutes and judgments for all Israel."

CHARACTERISTICS OF ZAYIN

Zacher = remember

REMEMBERING THE TORAH IS A GREAT SPIRITUAL WEAPON

Zayin is considered a crowned vav.

THE OVERSIZED ZAYIN

An oversized Zayin is found in Malachi 4:4.

FORM

Vav with a large "crown" on its head.

"Remember the Torah of Moses my servant that I commanded him at Horeb, the statues (chukim) and Judgements (mishpatim) for all Israel."

Since Zayin represents a weapon of the Spirit, remembering the Torah of Moses is here shown to be a great weapon to be used in spiritual warfare in our lives.

NUMBER

"All sevens are blessed (vayikra Rabbah 29:10) and the number seven has always been regarded in the Jewish tradition as the number of completion, wholeness, blessing, and rest.

THE WONDERFUL HEBREW ALPHABET 1 WORKBOOK

PICTURE

Sword and crown

NOTES:

_____

_____

_____

_____

_____

_____

_____

_____

_____

_____

ז ז ז ז ז

_____

_____

_____

_____

NOW YOU CAN SEE THE MYSTERY HIDDEN IN THE FIRST SEVEN LETTERS.

א The Father sent.

ב The master of the house who is.

ג The rich man to.

ד The poor man that he may.

ה Behold.

| The nail and

ז The crown!!

אבגדה|ז

The Father sent the master of the house who is YAHSHUAh the rich man to the poor man that he may behold the nail and the crown. Unless otherwise indicated, all scripture quotations are from the King James Version of the Bible.

99

BIBLIOGRAPHY

Grant Luton, *In His Own Words* John

J. Parsons, *Hebrew for Christians*

www.Chabad.Org

Jewish Encyclopedia

Www. Hiddentruthrevealed

J. R. Church & Gary Stearman, *The Mystery of the Menorah*

J.R. Chruch, *Hidden Prophecies in the Psalms*

Brad Scott, *www .wildbranch.org*

Benjamin Blech, *The Secrets of Hebrew Words*

The Chumash stone edition, Mesorah Publications, Ltd, Brooklyn New York Rabbi Michael L. Munk, *The Wisdom of the Hebrew Alphabet*